A Mouse In The House

A Mouse's Perception of the Insurrection

By R. E. Hogan

Illustrations by M. M. Powers

DEDICATION

This book is dedicated to
Officer Eugene Goodman
and all the other police officers
who protected our Capitol
and our democracy
on January 6, 2021.
You are true
American heroes.
We love and appreciate you
more than you know.

"History doesn't repeat itself, but it often rhymes."

--Mark Twain

“My name is Milton
Milton the mouse
This is my story
And the story of
The Peoples’ House.

You see, I live in the Capitol
Which stands in D. C.
I am here to do
My small/big part
To preserve and protect
Democracy.

So how did I get here?
You might rightly ask.
And what makes me think
I'm up to the task?

You see,
My family has always been political
Ever since World War II,
Starting way back in Europe
During the rise
Of their fascist coup.

My great-great grandfather
Lived with Hitler
In his chateau.
He witnessed his rageful rants
And the racial division
He effectively sowed.

1936
1936
JUNE
3

My great-great grandmother
A very pretty mouse,
I must say
Wandered into
Mussolini's garden
One bright sunny day.

There she heard the schemes
And the terrible lies
Of weak "strong" men
who wanted "others" to die.

After the war
My great-great grandparents
Met on a ship bound for the States.
They fell in love and got married
And together, they would strive
To fulfill their life's noble fate.

They settled in D.C.
This great nation's Capital
So they could take care of,
And watch over,
The United States of America.

They would do their small/big part
In the prevention of evil
In the prevention of fascism
And the needless killing
Of innocent people.

WELCOME TO
WASHINGTON, D.C.
NATION'S CAPITAL

And so, every generation of my family
Has lived in D.C.
We've done our small/big part
To preserve and protect
Democracy.

VOTE
ALL ARE
REATED
EQUAL
LOVE
ANOTHER!

We've all lived
In the Capitol Building
Mothers, fathers,
Daughters, sons
So here I am
On January sixth, twenty twenty-one.

2021
January
6
Good Morning! Congress is now in Session...
Cheese crackers

This was supposed to be
A normal, routine, boring day.
A bit of a yawn and a wink
and a, ‘Oh, you don't say?’

Follow me! We'll stop Them!
TRUMP

The politicians strolled
Into the chamber
With relative ease,
Not suspecting the Capitol
Would soon be under
A terrible siege

By the violent,
Rageful dangerous mob
Trying to prevent Congress
From doing it's job.

TRUN
Police

All was peaceful and calm
As the votes were to be cast,
When the silence was shattered
By the deafening sound
Of the breaking of glass.

I knew what this signaled
I knew what this was.
They were here to destroy
Democracy,
It's values . . . it's laws.

This treacherous sound
Had been heard years before,
As Nazis broke windows
In temples
And family-owned stores.

It was the sound of
Democracy
Cracking apart
And the sound of fascism
Attempting a violent new start.

2021
January
6
CRASH
Cheese crackers

My grandfather always said,
'Democracy is a fragile thing.
It needs lots and lots
Of care and protecting.'

2005
Jan.
30
..a fragile thing!

So when I heard the glass break
I jumped to my feet
And looked to the fly on the wall
I was sitting beneath.

I said, ‘Fly out there Frida
and see what you find.
I sense our democracy
is in a bit of a bind!’

So Frida flew out of the chamber
As fast as she could
Although she was tempted
To land on Mike's hair
As she passed where he stood.

She resisted temptation
And flew with intention
Out of the Chamber
Into dangerous sedition.

She was back in a flash
To report the destruction.
The lobby was trashed,
They were following
Deadly instructions.

XXX
XXX!X
XX

He had told a Big Lie
That tore the country apart.
He had won in a landslide
The mob believed in their hearts.

So they stormed the Capitol
That infamous day
And wreaked mayhem
And madness
To peoples' dismay.

TRU

I jumped on the shoulder
Of a secret service man
And whispered in his ear,
‘Get them to safety
While you still can!’

He moved them quite quickly
Away from the strife
And led them to safety
And out of plain sight.

EXIT

The mob did their damage
The vote, it was stalled.
Democracy faltered
But it did not fall.

For at the end of the day
The vote did take place.
Democracy stood strong
Despite the efforts
Of the radical base.

ELECTORIAL
COLLAGE
VOTES
COUNT

So let this be a lesson
To all of you,
Democracy can always
Be threatened
By a fascist coup.

Be alert, be on guard
And hear what I say,
We must be
Vigilant and diligent
For freedom to stay.

TODAYS NEWS

Don't think you're too young
Don't think you're too small.
Remember what a mouse and a fly
Could do when they answered
Democracy's call.

You decide
What happens from here.
Will love and equality
Replace violence and fear?

Will we love our neighbors
And be kind and good?
And treat them the way
Jesus would?

Congressman
R-ALABAMA
VOTER
SUPRESSION
BILL
Delete
RECONSTRUCTION
A History
of
Voter
supression
2021
NOVEMBER
6
EQUAL
RIGT

You're not too young
You're not too small
To hear the whisper
And answer
Democracy's call."

Questions and Answers

What is democracy?
Democracy is "a system of government by the whole population or all the eligible members of a state" ("Democratic Republic," 2021). In America, the people are represented by elected officials. Ideally, all members of the society are equal and are treated as such.

What is fascism?
Fascism is a system of government that is lead by a charismatic authoritarian all powerful leader that usually comes to power through violent means or manipulated elections. It frequently uses propaganda (lies), racism and scapegoating to inspire it's supporters to feel victimized in someway.

What is sedition?
Sedition is the act of "inciting a revolt or violence against a lawful authority" (Teka, 2021) or government "with the goal of destroying or overthrowing it" (Teka, 2021). The rally in D.C. prior to the attack on the Capitol was allegedly, an act of sedition as it incited the mob to commit acts of violence.

What is insurrection?
A violent uprising against an "authority or an established government" (Teka, 2021). The attack on the Capitol, on January 6, 2021, allegedly qualifies as an insurrection.

What is a coup?
"A sudden, violent, and illegal seizure of power from a government" (Oxford University Press (OUP), 2021). More specifically, America allegedly experienced an attempted Self-coup, which is when "a nation's leader, having come to power through legal means", attempts to stay in power unlawfully (Wikipedia contributors, 2021).

Who was Adolf Hitler?
Adolf Hitler was the fascist "dictator of Germany from 1933-1945" (Wikipedia contributors, 2021b). He "was the leader of the Nazi party" (Wikipedia contributors, 2021b). His beliefs in a master white race led to the mass murder of millions of non-Aryan people, especially those of Jewish descent. He also imprisoned or killed anyone who politically opposed him.

Who was Benito Mussolini?
Benito Mussolini, known as, "The Father of Fascism", was the fascist dictator of Italy from 1925-1945. He became an ally of Hitler's during World War II. Mussolini oversaw the murder of approximately 2000 political opponents within Italy and enacted anti-Semitic policies during World War II.

What is a "strong" man in this context?
A leader who rules by the exercise of threats, force, violence or blackmail.

What was Kristallnacht or the night of broken glass?
Kristallnacht refers to "November 9-10, 1938, when German Nazis attacked Jewish persons and property" (Berenbaum, 2020). This name refers to the "broken glass left in the streets after these" attacks (Berenbaum, 2020).

What is a scapegoat?
A scapegoat is a person, or in this case, a group of people blamed for all or most of the problems in a society. In Germany, during World War II, the Jews were scapegoated. In America, from 2016-2020 Mexicans and other Hispanic immigrants coming from South America were scapegoated. Scapegoating is frequently used to justify violence, incarceration or even genocide toward a group of people. Scapegoating allows a person or group of people to avoid taking responsibility for problems that have emerged within the society.

What is projection?
Projection is when a person or a group of people see or project their flawed characteristics or imperfections onto another person or group of people. An example of a projection is when members of the Republican party say that Democrats are “rigging" elections, while they themselves are allegedly trying to "rig" elections by attempting, as of this writing, to pass 250 laws in 43 states that are designed to suppress the votes of Democrats and people of color.

What is a "Big Lie"?
A "Big Lie" is an untruth told by a minority political group to their supporters, convincing them that they have been cheated in some way. If the Lie is big enough, it has supporters question and lose faith in established institutions, elected officials, and the election process. It then becomes the fertile ground for false conspiracy theories. The "Big Lie" is told repeatedly to manipulate supporters and stoke violent action in order to gain power. "Stop the Steal" is allegedly an example of a Big Lie.

What is gaslighting?
Gaslighting is a form of covert manipulation that occurs in abusive relationships. The bully or abuser makes the target question their judgment and reality. It is a form of emotional abuse based on repeated lies intended to mislead and stoke fear. The term refers to the 1944 movie, "Gaslight", in which this type of manipulation and abuse occurred. After 63 court cases ruled that the 2020 election was free and fair, repeatedly saying the election was rigged and stolen is not only an example of an alleged Big Lie, but it is also an example of "gaslighting" Americans.

Who participates in a democracy?
Ideally, everyone participates in a democracy by voting and by taking peaceful actions to support the issues and candidates they believe in.

How can you do your small/big part?
You can support our democracy, by registering and voting when you turn 18 years old and by simply treating everyone with respect, dignity, love and kindness regardless of their age, gender, race or political party. Also, stay informed and keep up with both national and local current events. Make sure your news sources are reputable. You may even discover something that you love to do such as drawing, writing, teaching etc. that supports our democracy. Remember, democracy requires participation and you can make a difference!

References

Berenbaum, M. (2020, November 2). Kristallnacht | Definition, Date, Facts, & Significance. Encyclopedia Britannica. https://www.britannica.com/event/Kristallnacht

Democratic republic. (2021, June 19). In Wikipedia. https://en.wikipedia.org/wiki/Democratic_republic#:%7E:text=Republic%3A%20%22A%20state%20in%20which,%2C%20typically%20through%20elected%20representatives.%22

Insurrection. (2021). The Merriam-Webster.Com Dictionary. https://www.merriam-webster.com/dictionary/insurrection

Oxford University Press (OUP). (2021). coup. Lexico.Com. https://www.lexico.com/en/definition/coup

Teka, M., Esq. (2021, January 8). Sedition. Findlaw. https://www.findlaw.com/criminal/criminal-charges/sedition.html

Wikipedia contributors. (2021, June 10). Self-coup. Wikipedia. https://en.wikipedia.org/wiki/Self-coup

Wikipedia contributors. (2021b, June 13). Adolf Hitler. Wikipedia. https://en.wikipedia.org/wiki/Adolf_Hitler

About the Author

R. E. Hogan is an international, award winning published poet. Who also authored the Children's book, "The Little Tree Who Didn't Want to be Green".

About the illustrator

M. M. Powers. ”Art has always been a comfort and a joy for me.”

www.ingramcontent.com/pod-product-compliance
Ingram Content Group UK Ltd.
Pitfield, Milton Keynes, MK11 3LW, UK
UKHW060116300726
14090UKWH00002B/225

* 9 7 9 8 5 2 1 7 5 8 6 5 4 *